DEBBIE MACOMBER

PATTERNS *of* GRACE

DEVOTIONS
FROM THE HEART

Guideposts

Patterns of Grace

ISBN 978-0-8249-4533-6

Published by Guideposts
16 East 34th Street
New York, NY 10016
Guideposts.org

Distributed by Ideals Publications, a Guideposts company
2630 Elm Hill Pike, Suite 100
Nashville, TN 37214

Guideposts and *Ideals* are registered trademarks of Guideposts.

Acknowledgments

Every attempt has been made to credit the sources of copyrighted material used in this book. If any such acknowledgment has been inadvertently omitted or miscredited, receipt of such information would be appreciated.

Scripture references are from the following sources: The Holy Bible, King James Version (KJV). The Holy Bible, New King James Version (NKJV). Copyright © 1997, 1990, 1985, 1983 by Thomas Nelson, Inc. The Holy Bible, New International Version®, NIV®. Copyright © 1973, 1978, 1984 by Biblica, Inc.™ Used by permission of Zondervan. All rights reserved worldwide. The Revised Standard Version Bible (RSV), copyright © 1946, 1952, and 1971 National Council of the Churches of Christ in the United States of America. Used by permission. All rights reserved. The Holy Bible, New Living Translation (NLT), copyright 1996, 2004 by Tyndale House Foundation. Used by permission of Tyndale House Publishers, Inc., Carol Stream, Illinois 60188. *The Message* (MSG). Copyright © 1993, 1994, 1995, 1996, 2000, 2001, 2002 by Eugene Peterson. Used by permission of NavPress, Colorado Springs, CO. *The Living Bible* (TLB) © 1971. Used by permission of Tyndale House Publishers, Inc., Carol Stream, Illinois 60188. The New Century Version® (NCV). Copyright © 1987, 1988, 1991, 2005 by Thomas Nelson, Inc. Used by permission. All rights reserved.

Cover and interior design by David Carlson | Studio Gearbox
Cover photograph by Corbis Photography
Typeset by Jeff Jansen | Aesthetic Soup

Printed in China
10 9 8 7 6 5 4 3 2 1

Contents

Introduction

I'm a shameless knitter, and part of the enjoyment I receive from knitting is looking at patterns. I'll find one that looks like a fun knit, do a search through my accumulated stash for the perfect yarn and then reach for my knitting needles.

Over the years I've been an eyewitness to the patterns God has woven into my life. I've written about them. Sometimes God's hand is obvious and at other times He can be understated and subtle, patiently waiting for me to acknowledge Him working behind the scenes. To me these are patterns of grace. God's grace.

These devotions were originally printed by Guideposts in the annual devotional book they publish, *Daily Guideposts*. I'd read this devotional for years and came to know the writers like family. In a manner of speaking they are my family; my Christian family. Then I met one of these writers, Mary Lou Carney, on a chance encounter—but really, is anything by chance when God is involved? Mary Lou encouraged me to submit my own devotions, which I did, and as they say, the rest is...an entire book titled *Patterns of Grace*.

My prayer is that this book will bless you in your own walk with the Lord, that upon examination you will recognize God's hand in your life... patterns of grace that He has lavished upon you.

No project such as this is accomplished as a sole effort. My appreciation is extended first and foremost to Wendy Lawton, who is far more than my nonfiction agent and a God friend. Without her organizational skills I fear this book wouldn't have been possible. Also I owe appreciation to Andrew Attaway, the Guideposts editor who guided me through the devotional writing process. And to Rebecca Maker, the editor for *Patterns of Grace*. My husband Wayne, who is ever patient with me, and our children and grandchildren, who are often the instruments God uses to teach me lessons on grace.

Enjoy.

Debbie Macomber

March 2012

CHAPTER 1

Follow Your Dreams

God created us to dream. When we fail to dream, we rob Him of the opportunity to do great things. Sometimes we shy away from dreaming big dreams. Maybe we don't want to ask for too much. Maybe we somehow don't feel worthy. But over and over again in the Bible, the Lord instructs us to envision what He can do. Our job is to dream.

I can do all things through Christ
who strengthens me.

—PHILIPPIANS 4:13 (NKJV)

I grew up in Yakima, Washington, with a large extended family. We cousins were as close as brothers and sisters; we lived in the same neighborhood, attended the same church and school and often vacationed together.

After I married Wayne and moved to Kent, just a few miles south of Seattle, my cousin David, who was closest to me in age, developed leukemia. His doctors sent him to Seattle's Fred Hutchinson Cancer Research Center. Although I didn't often venture into the big city, I was determined to visit David.

Somehow I ended up at Swedish Hospital, which is connected to Fred Hutchinson by a sky bridge. Lost and confused, I wandered down a number of corridors without finding the bridge. Finally, I stopped a doctor and asked if he could give me directions.

"It's simple," he assured me. "All you need to do is walk down this hallway, take the first right and walk through the door marked ABSOLUTELY NO ADMITTANCE."

Those directions did more than show me the way to my cousin. Somehow, that experience has given me the courage to walk through other doors: my dyslexia that I feared would keep me from working; my terror of speaking in front of people. God has met me at the door marked ABSOLUTELY NO ADMITTANCE and held it open for me.

Father God, thank You for the obstacles You send into my life that have taught me to rely only on You.

One of my favorite verses

Great is his faithfulness; his mercies begin afresh each morning.

LAMENTATIONS 3:23 (NLT)

Like arrows in the hands of a warrior
are sons born in one's youth.
Blessed is the man whose quiver is full of them.

—PSALM 127:4 5 (NIV)

My husband Wayne and I were blessed with four children in a five-year span. By the time Dale, our youngest, was born, I hadn't slept through the night in three long years. The house was in constant chaos, and in those pre–disposable diaper days, the washing machine was going day and night. My hands were more than full with the demands of our growing family. Thankfully, I was blessed with wonderful parents who visited us often. Soon after Dale's arrival, my mother came to help.

Early one morning, when our newborn woke for his feeding, his older sisters and brother came looking for

attention. Jody sat on one knee and Jenny on the other, and Ted shared space with his infant brother on my lap. All too soon, the older three started squabbling and whining.

My mother woke up and joined us in the living room. "Oh, Debbie," she said with a smile, "these are the happiest days of your life." Aghast, I looked at her and said, "Mom, you mean it gets worse?"

Now, in retrospect, I can see how very blessed I was. Mom had the perspective to see it then; thank God, I can see it now.

Lord, give all parents the patience, the prayer and the sense of humor they need to raise their children in Your grace.

You are the provider of my life,
but just as in the story of the loaves
and the fishes, You often require
something to work with. Something
willingly surrendered from me.
Let me give You my heart, Lord.
Start there, but then work with
my stubbornness, my pride,
my weakness—and mold me
into someone whose life and
words could feed multitudes.

One of my favorite verses

I strain to reach the end of the race and receive the prize for which
God through Christ Jesus is calling us up to heaven.

PHILIPPIANS 3:14 (NLT)

*I will show you what he is like who comes to me
and hears my words and puts them into practice.*

—LUKE 6:47 (NIV)

Every New Year's Day I ask the Lord to give me a word to focus on for the next twelve months. It doesn't always come to me right away, but I keep my mind and my heart open and wait. Generally, within a week or two the word presents itself. Instantly, I know it's the right one, and I ask God to use it to teach me the lessons I need to learn in the coming year.

This year as I prayed, my heart was heavy. My father has been seriously ill for a long while and was recently placed in a nursing home. My prayers were clouded with worries about what the future held for him and for my mother. Then it came to me that my word was *surrender*. The Lord was asking me to surrender my father to Him,

13

to give Him all my worries and fears. It wasn't the word I wanted.

As I drove to meet my walking partner for our morning walk, my eyes clouded with tears as I tried to imagine life without my dad. But as I drove past the Sun Trust bank, I blinked in amazement. Through my tears, the sign outside seemed to read SON TRUST. I stopped the car. Now I was sure God was asking me to put my trust in Him, to surrender my will to His. It wouldn't be easy, but I knew that He would provide the grace required for the task.

Oh, Father, how grateful I am for Your promises.
I surrender myself to Your precious will.

One of my favorite verses

Your Word is a lamp for my feet and a light for my path.

PSALM 119:105 (NLT)

Be strong and courageous. Do not be terrified;
do not be discouraged, for the LORD your God
will be with you wherever you go.

—JOSHUA 1:9 (NIV)

It had been a difficult year for my husband Wayne and me. Our youngest son had received two DUI tickets. We'd poured out our hearts to God and prayed He would work in Dale's life. Once Dale entered rehab, we assumed everything would get better. Instead, everything seemed to get worse. Dale lost his job and took one personal blow after another. He was sober, but nothing else seemed to change.

I'm most comfortable writing out my prayers, and day after day I poured out my heart on paper to the Lord, praying for Dale. As matters grew worse, I began to doubt

that God was listening or that He even cared. Why was He allowing all this to come down on our son when he was working so hard to get his life in order? It made no sense.

Then one morning after we'd received more bad news from Dale, my pen refused to work. I couldn't write out my prayers; it was as if God were tired of hearing from me. I must have mumbled something to myself because Wayne came to check on me. Shaking the pen in frustration, I told him my pen wouldn't work. Calmly, Wayne poured a glass of hot water and set the pen inside. When I picked it up again, the ink flowed smoothly. I stared at it for a long time, and with tears in my eyes I recognized what God was attempting to tell me: He was working in Dale's life. He's set our son in hot water so that Dale can work out his issues. Everything was happening just the way God meant it to.

Thank You, Father, that You hear our prayers.
Thank You, too, for the lesson that a little hot water
is exactly what Dale needed.

Dear Lord, have Your way with me. My heart is filled with encouragement and hope this morning that Your love is deep enough, wide enough, high enough to compensate for all my flaws and stubborn pride. I am Your daughter, and it never ceases to amaze me that my God could love me.

There is a battle raging in me, Lord. A huge battle.
A continual struggle as I head across this desert of testing.
My eyes are focused on the Promised Land but my heart falters
and longs for Egypt. Help me, Lord. My heart is Yours.
My heart, my life, my will, my all—it belongs to You!

Your love, LORD, reaches to the heavens,
your faithfulness to the skies.

—PSALM 36:5 (NIV)

A few years ago, a friend gave me a gold cross hand-crafted by her mother. I treasured that cross and took special care of it. Then one day I couldn't find it. I made a careful search for it, but to no avail.

The missing cross weighed on my mind for weeks, until one Saturday I decided I'd look for it and wouldn't give up until I found it. That morning, as I finished my prayers, I reached for pen and paper and wrote a letter to the Lord, reminding Him how much I loved the cross and asking Him to help me find it. After I'd written two pages, I put aside the prayer letter and began my search.

The logical place to start was my jewelry box, even though I'd looked there many times before. I opened it and removed all the necklaces. There, in the back, was the cross. I was stunned. After weeks of worry and fruitless searching, I found it in the first place I looked.

I clenched the cross in my hand, closed my eyes and prayed a prayer of thanksgiving. Then I heard an answer in my heart.

"Debbie," the voice said, "all you had to do was ask."

God, I don't know why I turn to You as a last resort
when You should be the first one I seek.
Every time I wear this cross, remind me of Your faithfulness.

It just came to me, dear Lord,
that holiness is obedience.
Every time I turn away from my
weakness and look instead to You,
I am practicing the art of holiness.
Discipline—especially that which
involves self—is a form of worship.
I can say I love You and want
to serve You, but without obedience
these are empty words.

> Let us then approach the throne of grace
> with confidence.
>
> —HEBREWS 4:16 (NIV)

My grandson Cameron loves to play soldier, so for his ninth birthday his mother—my daughter Jenny—decided to give him a military-themed party. The invitations were draft notices, and my son-in-law designed an obstacle course for the ten boys who were to attend. My oldest son Ted, who'd served as an Airborne Ranger, painted camouflage on the boys' faces, and they ate MREs in the field. (For us civilians, that's meals ready to eat.) The party was a huge success.

Later that summer, Cameron spent an entire day outside arranging his toy soldiers. When he'd finished, he insisted his mother take a picture, just in case she happened to meet a general. How or when this was supposed to occur was of little concern to my grandson. He instructed his mother to hand over the picture so that the army could make use of his battle plan.

I enjoyed telling my husband about Cameron's exploits, and I have to admit that we were both impressed. Even at the age of nine, he felt he had something of value to offer others. *We all do,* I thought later, *whether it's a shared recipe or an unexpected birthday card to a shut-in or even what we're convinced is a brilliant business plan.*

So I've made Cameron's message my own: Believe in yourself and in God's ability to use your talents as He sees fit.

Lord, thank You for the lesson in self-confidence
that my grandson has taught me.

Dearest Father, use me! Take me, flawed as I am, and use my talents, strengths, my weaknesses and all that I am to spread the word of Your love to others. To those incarcerated, to those bound at home and to those with little joy in their lives—allow me to touch their lives for You.

In you they trusted and were not disappointed.

—PSALM 22:5 (NIV)

Several years ago, inspired by a book I'd read, I made a list of thirty people I hoped to meet one day. The list was wide and varied, including writers, motivational speakers and celebrities. Amazingly, over the last several years, I've met eighteen people on that list. Some of them were everything I'd expected, and others were major disappointments.

Not long ago, after one such disappointment, I was complaining to God about how disillusioned I'd been. Then God spoke to me in my heart: *Debbie, you asked to meet these people and I'm happy to send them into your life, but I want you to make another list.*

"Another list?"

This time, leave the spaces blank. I'm going to send thirty people into

29

your life whom I want you to meet, and I promise you none of them will be a disappointment.

This prayer-time conversation has had a curious effect on me. Now, whenever I meet someone, I look at him or her with fresh eyes and wonder if this is one of the people God is sending into my life. I find that I'm more open, more receptive, waiting expectantly for those God wants me to meet. Since then, I've been blessed in countless ways. I've still got my original list, but it's not nearly as important to me as the one God asked me to keep.

Father, thank You for the special people You have sent into my life. Not a single one has ever disappointed me.

One of my favorite verses

*For these commands and this teaching
are a lamp to light the way ahead of you.*

PROVERBS 6:23 (NLT)

Dearest Jesus, help me to be faithful to You this day in all I say and do, in all my thoughts and actions. Don't allow me to get bogged down in the "if onlys" of life. Make my heart pure so that I can serve You. Help me to be the woman You've always intended me to be.

> I will also give him a white stone with a new name
> written on it, known only to him who receives it.

—REVELATION 2:17 (NIV)

M̲y friend Sheila invited me to lunch to discuss what
wasn't happening in her career. She needed to
increase her income, but nothing she'd tried had worked
out. She felt a sense of panic because her son had headed
off to college and she'd promised to cover his expenses.
With nothing more profitable on the horizon, she took on
a teaching assignment while continuing to look around. I
encouraged her as best I could.

The next time we met, Sheila was beaming and I
was certain she had good news to tell me. She announced
that she had changed her name. She noticed in the Bible
that every time God was ready to do a mighty work in

someone's life, He changed the person's name: Abram became Abraham, Sarai became Sarah, Simon became Peter, Saul became Paul. Sheila announced that her new name was Sheila the Faithful.

Amazingly, although her career didn't progress until after her son graduated from college, she was able to meet every single tuition payment.

Sheila inspired me so much that I decided to change my name too. I thought about becoming Debbie, God's Patient Daughter, but that just seemed to be asking for trouble. Debbie the Generous had a nice sound to it; I was sure a generous heart would be pleasing to God. Then, as I was praying for my son Dale, burdened by some of his recent decisions, it came to me: God was asking me to trust Him. So I released Dale into God's hands and became Debbie the Trusting.

Thank You, Jesus, for special friends whose examples of walking in faith inspire me to walk along with them.

One of my favorite verses

Whatever you do, do well.

Ecclesiastes 9:10 (NLT)

Good morning, Lord. May compassion for others become my passion. Never allow me to look upon one less fortunate than myself and feel nothing. Never allow my heart to become so calloused that I don't hurt when one of Your children hurt. Let Your own compassion be my compassion. You shed Your blood for me. You bled all along the road to Calvary for me.

Ask and it will be given to you; seek and you will find;
knock and the door will be opened to you.
For everyone who asks receives; he who seeks finds;
and to him who knocks, the door will be opened.

— MATTHEW 7:7–8 (NIV)

For as long as I can remember, I've made lists. There's a list for what I need to pick up at the grocery store, a daily appointment schedule; I've even taken time to think well into the future with five- and ten-year goals.

When our children lived at home, I wrote up goal worksheets for them. Every January 1, we sat around the dining room table, filled out the worksheets and read the ones from the previous year. The tradition continues: My husband Wayne and I spend part of the first day of the year talking about the twelve months ahead. We chat about commitments we've already made and set time aside for people we want to see and places we plan to visit. We have financial goals, recreational ones, personal goals and spiritual ones. It's our way of laying out the year before God, telling Him the things we'd like to accomplish and asking for His blessing in order to see them come to pass.

This last time, though, I had trouble focusing on my goals. Naturally, I want everything I do to be wildly successful, but so many factors are in play that the final outcome is completely out of my control. Some of my goals seemed more like wishes.

Then one day, shortly after the first of the year, I drove past a billboard that read: SOME THINGS NEED TO BE BELIEVED IN ORDER TO BE SEEN.

I have a new category for my goal worksheets now: "Needs to Be Believed." It's a list that's growing longer every year.

Father God, thank You for the dreams
You've planted in my heart.

One of my favorite verses

Live creatively, friends.... Make a careful exploration of who you are and the work you have been given, and then sink yourself into that. Don't be impressed with yourself. Don't compare yourself with others. Each of you must take responsibility for doing the creative best you can with your own life.

GALATIANS 6: 1, 4–5 (MSG)

Say Yes to Your Dreams

"Honey, you need to find a job." It was early 1980 and my husband Wayne stood in the kitchen doorway, clutching a handful of unpaid bills. My stomach clenched and I swallowed an automatic protest before I saw the look of regret in his eyes. We were going deeper into debt each month while I struggled to sell my first novel.

For as long as I could remember, I dreamed of writing novels. My love for the written word started early, when my mother took me to the library for story hour. From the time I was three years old, I went to sleep at night with a book in my hands. I discovered the powerful connection between the story and the reader. I could feel what the characters felt, cry with them, laugh with them. I wanted to write stories like that. I dreamed of the day when readers would hold my book in their hands.

You might be surprised to know that reading didn't come easy to me. I was the only girl in my first-grade class to be in the robin (slow) reading group. It turned out that I was dyslexic, but back in the early 1950s my teachers didn't have a word for it. I can remember my third-grade teacher telling my mother, "Debbie is such a nice girl, but she'll never do well in school." To this day I'm a slow, thoughtful reader and a creative speller.

Nevertheless, the dream persisted. I wanted to write books. When Wayne and I married and had our four children in quick succession, it was easy to stuff my dreams into the future with a long list of justifications and excuses. Then a dear cousin died suddenly. It felt as if God was saying to me that if I was ever going to write, the time was now. Life is short. Get started.

We rented a typewriter and I put it on the kitchen table. The kids would go out the door to school and Super Mom was transformed into that hopeful young writer. For two and a half years I sat at that kitchen table and pounded away on those typewriter keys, completing two full novels. Because I was doing something I loved, I was genuinely happy. Because I was pursuing a lifelong dream, I was a better wife and better mother.

*For as long as I could remember,
I dreamed of writing novels. My love for
the written word started early, when my mother
took me to the library for story hour.*

But everything came to a crashing halt that Sunday afternoon. Wayne set down the unpaid bills. Together we reviewed our finances and I realized there wasn't any alternative. I had to get a job, a real job, that would contribute to our family income.

With the newspaper in hand, I circled three positions to apply for the next morning. Even if I was fortunate enough to get hired right away, I'd be lucky to receive anything above minimum wage.

As I looked up from the newspaper, my gaze fell on the typewriter and I knew this would be the end of my dream of selling a novel. All four children were involved in sports, music, Scouts and church. There simply weren't enough hours in the day for me to keep up with the kids' schedules, work full-time, maintain the house and still write. I might as well kiss that dream good-bye.

What was the use anyway? Really, what chance did I have of selling a novel? Everyone said I had to know someone if I was ever to get published—an editor, an agent, someone in the business. I didn't, and that was just one more strike against me.

Doubts battered me as I considered those three want ads. There wasn't anything wrong with any of them, except that I had no desire to work as a receptionist or a cashier. I was born to tell stories—only now that dream had to be dashed.

I went to bed that night and tried not to let Wayne know how depressed I was. In the darkness, with Wayne sleeping beside me, I remembered the enthusiasm with which I'd started out on this venture. Despite everything, I had felt so sure God was leading me to write. I was willing to tackle every obstacle. With my Bible and a copy of Norman Vincent Peale's *The Power of Positive Thinking* at my side, I had been certain that sooner or later a New York publisher would recognize my talent.

Here I was, two and a half years into the journey and I hadn't sold a single word. Instead of contributing to our family finances, I was draining them. My dream was simply too expensive.

I tossed and turned miserably. Finally, in desperation, I silently called out to God. *Lord, You gave me this dream in the first place and I've gone as far as I can with it. I'm giving it back. The rest is up to You.*

About two or three in the morning, Wayne rolled over. "Are you awake?"

"I haven't been to sleep yet," I said.

He waited a moment and then asked, "What's wrong?"

My heart was so heavy that I blurted out the truth. "You know, I really think I could have made it as a writer."

Wayne didn't say anything for a long time. Then he sat up and turned on the light. An eternity passed before he said, "All right, honey, go for it. We'll make whatever sacrifices we need to make. We'll figure it out. Don't worry."

I am forever grateful to my husband for rescuing my dream. How fortunate I am that Wayne believed so strongly in me and my talent.

I wish I could tell you it was only a matter of a few weeks before New York recognized my talent and offered me that first contract. It was another two and a half years of financial struggles before I sold a manuscript. I faced one challenge after another. The most humbling came at a writers' conference where my manuscript was picked to be reviewed by a real New York book editor. She had the entire room laughing at the implausibility of my plot. Afterward, I went to her and asked if she'd be willing to look at the manuscript again if I rewrote it. She looked me in the eye, leaned forward and, placing her hand on my arm, said, "Throw it away."

I loved this story and the characters, and refused to believe that it deserved to be discarded. Instead I submitted it elsewhere. Then in 1982 the long-awaited phone call came from New York. I was going to be a published author! Soon after, I wrote Dr. Peale and thanked him for writing *The Power of Positive*

Thinking. His book was instrumental in helping me hold on to my dream. "I believe God plants dreams in our hearts so we'll learn to turn to Him, to trust Him to see them to fruition," I wrote. To my absolute delight Dr. Peale wrote me back with more encouragement. It meant as much to me as any advice I've ever gotten from an editor.

Not long ago I discovered a spiral-bound journal. The first entry read: *January 1, 1973: Since the greatest desire of my life is to somehow, some way, be a writer, I'll start with the pages of this journal.*

A dream is a journey that begins with a single step and the belief that you will be led faithfully along the way.

Dearest Lord,

I know that dreams are often straight from You.

Through our dreams,

You give us the vision of how we can develop our

uniqueness and use our gifts for You.

I believe so strongly in the power of dreams.

All my life I felt it was You who gave me

the dream of being a writer,

planting it deep in my heart,

nurturing it from the time I was a child,

keeping it alive in those dark years.

May my words touch lives for You.

Help us all to dream big dreams.

Amen.

CHAPTER 2

God's Handiwork

When my grandchildren were little, there was nothing as
sweet as seeing their little fingerprints all over the glass of
my windows. It reminded me that they had been there,
leaving their precious mark on my windows and my heart.
In the same way, God has left His fingerprints on my life.
The Bible tells me that He knit me together in my mother's
womb. His handiwork—His fingerprints—are part of the
very fiber of our lives.

My dear brothers and sisters, be strong
and immovable. Always work enthusiastically
for the Lord, for you know that nothing you do
for the Lord is ever useless.

—1 CORINTHIANS 15:58 (NLT)

I've long believed that God sends people into our lives.
Sometimes I don't recognize them as quickly as I should;
at other times it's so obvious I can't ignore it. This past year
I had the privilege of meeting Kent Annan, a missionary
to Haiti.

I first heard about Kent from a friend, an avowed
agnostic who'd read Kent's book *Following Jesus through the
Eye of the Needle* and knew I'd enjoy the story. I ordered the
book and started to read it in fits and starts.

Then a month later someone else mentioned Kent's

name and mailed me a second copy of the book. By this point I'd gotten the message: God wanted me to read the book. I did and was deeply touched by the powerful message. Then to my surprise I discovered that Kent Annan lived just a few miles from me. I got in touch with him, and the two of us met for lunch.

As we shared the meal, Kent told me that his father was a pastor. Kent had lived a pretty normal life before his call to the mission field. He'd never rebelled against his family or his God. His spiritual life, Kent said, had been filled with "little conversions," small steps of faith that drew him closer to God and lit his own life path.

I thought about what Kent shared that day and realized I've had little conversions too. They were the quiet mornings when I prayed and felt His presence and His love, guiding me, urging me to step forward in faith and assuring me He would always be at my side.

Thank You, Father, for Your presence and peace,
and for the confidence in knowing that You are always with me.

One of my favorite verses

God's Word is alive and is sharper than a double-edged sword.
It cuts all the way into us, where the soul and the spirit
are joined, to the center of our joints and bones. And it judges
the thoughts and feelings in our hearts.

HEBREWS 4:12 (NCV)

*The wolf will live with the lamb, the leopard will
lie down with the goat, the calf and the lion and the
yearling together; and a little child will lead them.*

—Isaiah 11:6 (NIV)

A few years back I was seated on a plane next to a
teenage boy who was the talkative sort. We struck up
a conversation and chatted for a good portion of the flight.
I talked to him about my work and then showed him my
current knitting project. Both are passions of mine, along
with my family.

Although we'd been talking the entire flight, I didn't
really know what his passions were. He was a rather cheerful
young man and, like our younger son, he was a runner, and
was active in his school and church, but little else. So I asked
him what his passion was.

He turned and looked at me and didn't answer for several moments. "I only have one real passion," he told me.

I sat up to take notice.

"Jesus Christ," he said. "I want to share what Christ did for me with everyone I meet."

I learned a valuable lesson from that young man: My life may be filled with passions, but none are as important as my relationship with my Savior.

Lord, thank You for the passions in my life,
but don't ever let me forget that You are first and foremost.

Work on me, dear Father!
I feel as though I am under
construction, made with the most
perfect supplies, crafted in the image
of the Almighty God Himself—
built up with all the saints,
fitted for Your honor and glory.
Make me worthy to serve You!

> "Haven't you read," he replied, "that at the
> beginning the Creator 'made them male
> and female,' and said, 'For this reason a man
> will leave his father and mother and be united to his
> wife, and the two will become one flesh?'
> So they are no longer two, but one."
>
> —MATTHEW 19:4–6 (NIV)

There are no two ways about it: My husband Wayne and I are about as different as any two people can be. He's introspective and quiet; I thrive on being around people. When we met, it was just he and his mother, whereas I came from a large extended family with lots of cousins. He's a night owl, and I'm a morning person.

For the last thirty-seven years, for the most part, we've managed to love and accept each other's strengths and weaknesses. There are times, however, when I can't help being frustrated with him.

Last week, I wanted to go to a movie, but he didn't. We stayed home. I wanted to invite friends over for dinner; the two of us ended up watching television. An exhibit on 9/11 had come to Tacoma: I wanted to go; Wayne didn't. Frustrated, I went without him, grumbling the entire way.

I wasn't quite done being upset when I was dressing for church the following morning. After the singing—I sang, Wayne didn't—the pastor began his sermon.

I don't remember the topic; in fact, I don't think I can even tell you which Bible passage he was preaching on. But at one point he said, "The grass isn't greener on the other side of the fence. It's greener where it's watered."

Wayne looked at me and I looked at him. He smiled and so did I. I offered my husband my hand, and we scooted just a bit closer to each other. We'd both heard something we needed to hear.

Lord, thank You for my husband,
for his quiet strength and his love.

One of my favorite verses

The LORD is good. When trouble comes he is a strong refuge.
And he knows everyone who trusts in him.

NAHUM 1:7 (NLT)

I have a keen interest in unusual street names. In fact, I'm on the lookout for street signs whenever my husband Wayne and I get in the car.

One of my favorites is Baby Doll Road, which isn't far from where we live. There's a road called Noisy Hole in Mashpee, Massachusetts, and another named Succabone in Bedford Hills, New York. One that made me sit up and take notice was Hell for Certain Road in Hyden, Kentucky. I can't say what kind of people live there, but the name certainly got my attention.

Just recently in our own hometown of Port Orchard, Washington, Wayne and I drove past a street sign that I'd never noticed before. It was on a road I normally travel two or three times a week, and not once had this sign caught my attention: EASY STREET.

"Quick," I told Wayne, pointing to the sign, "take a right."

He cast me a befuddled look. "Whatever for?"

"I want to see the houses of the people who live on Easy Street." I wasn't sure what to expect, but it wouldn't hurt to take a look. I wasn't really surprised to find that the homes looked very much like those in other neighborhoods close by. But as we wound our way down Easy Street, Wayne and I made a startling discovery: It was a dead end.

Lord, sometimes I'm guilty of wanting to live on Easy Street. Thank You for leading me down the path that leads to You.

Dearest Father,
I long to leap with sure feet
from one mountain of faith
experience to another.
Let me always start
and end with You.
Guide me through this day, Father.
Walk with me, teach me to leap,
help me to grow.
Encourage and fortify me
forever as Your child.

One of my favorite verses

But as for me, I know that my Redeemer lives
and he will stand upon the earth at last.

JOB 19:25 (NLT)

ss. Renée on a
ndi un ma
. Papa desire
ve la lecture
l faut just te
s envoie a
citebus s

A friend loves at all times.

PROVERBS 17:17 (RSV)

I'd always been a stay-at-home mom, working as time allowed, but when my children were grown, my goal was to get out of the house and become part of the business community. After ten years of working hard from home, I proudly signed my name to a lease for my own office and found myself facing hard decisions in a world completely foreign to me.

I knew I needed help, but where was I going to get it? As a first step, I contacted some successful businesswomen in our town—Lillian, a lawyer; Betty, a bank vice president; Diana, a social worker; Stephanie, a business owner; and Janelle, a real estate broker. I invited them to tea and asked their advice. We had such a good time together that we decided to meet every Thursday for breakfast.

That was eight years ago, and we still meet every Thursday to encourage and support one another. We bring our pains and our triumphs to breakfast; seek advice and share our troubles freely. We wept together when Stephanie developed cancer and died within five short months, and celebrated when Betty, a widow, met a wonderful man and remarried. We laugh together and cry together—often at the same time.

The years have seen many changes in our lives, but what started out as an easy way for me to learn more about being a good businesswoman has evolved into something far more powerful: friendship, and a blessing from God.

Thank You, Lord, for the special friends
You've brought into my life. May we always continue
to be close to You and to one another.

One of my favorite verses

*For God has not given us a spirit of timidity but of love,
power and self-discipline.*

2 TIMOTHY 1:7 (NLT)

O LORD, you are my God; I will exalt you
and praise your name, for in perfect faithfulness you
have done marvelous things, things planned long ago.

—ISAIAH 25:1 (NIV)

As I grow older, I've come to recognize God's hand in my life more and more. For instance, the night I met Wayne, I had a date who canceled at the last moment. I was dressed and ready to go, only to have my plans dashed. No more than a half hour later the phone rang again; it was a friend of my roommate's who was looking for a date to take to a movie. That was how I met my husband.

This last summer something occurred that had God's fingerprints all over it. I was in Phoenix on tour with a number of events scheduled. My travel plans are arranged a year in advance and my schedule on the road is usually jam-packed, but for some inexplicable reason, that particular morning was open.

As it happened, the son of one of our dearest friends was to be buried that day in Phoenix and his funeral was that morning. I'm convinced that God knew and prepared the way for me to attend Michael's funeral. I was able to be in church to love, support and comfort our friends.

God's intervention is evident in every corner of my life; I call these "divine appointments." Often, I don't recognize these intersections of time and eternity until much later. It takes what seems to be happenstance to show me once again that He is in control of every detail.

Open my eyes, Lord Jesus, to Your divine appointments.

Dear Lord,
plant me in solid ground.
Sink the roots of my faith
in the vitamin-rich soil of Your love.
Water my faith with Your Word;
cultivate and weed me
with Your call to divine obedience.
When the produce comes,
Lord, may it be abundant and full.

> For John baptized with water, but...you will be
> baptized with the Holy Spirit.
>
> —ACTS 1:5 (NIV)

Something strange has been happening to me in the last few years: I cry in church. For no reason that I can understand or explain, right in the middle of worship my eyes will cloud with tears. I blink furiously and take deep, even breaths to keep them at bay, but it rarely helps. My husband Wayne has gotten into the habit of carrying a handkerchief with him on Sunday morning. Apparently, he recognizes the signs now, because halfway through the service he tucks the hankie into my hand and gives my fingers a gentle squeeze.

If those tears in church weren't embarrassing enough, the same thing started happening during my morning prayer time. I'm most comfortable communicating with

God in writing, but these days many of my prayers are smudged with tears. I was convinced that this was a side effect of menopause, but that didn't seem to affect anything other than my worship and prayer time.

My friend Wendy came to visit recently. I casually mentioned how easily the tears flowed when I communicated with God. She smiled knowingly. "That happens to me too."

"It does?"

She nodded. "Those tears are an indication that the Holy Spirit has touched me in some way."

I pondered her words for a long time and recognized the truth in them. My tears in church don't embarrass me any longer; they're my emotional response to the overwhelming love of God as He touches my heart with His Spirit.

Holy Spirit, sweep down over Your people
and touch our hearts that we might serve God. Amen.

My heart seeks You for comfort,
guidance, assurance and love,
dear Lord. As I walk through
this desert of testing, I ask that
not only will You guide me
with a pillar of fire but that You
will walk at my side and whisper
encouragement in my ear.

One of my favorite verses

And this is the will of God, that I should not lose even one of all those he has given me, but that I should raise them up at the last day.

JOHN 6:39 (NLT)

The fruit of the Spirit is love, joy,
peace, patience, kindness, goodness,
faithfulness, gentleness and self-control.

—GALATIANS 5:22 (NIV)

I've heard it said that after many years of married life,
couples start to look like each other. I don't know if
that's true in Wayne's and my case. However, I can state
that an amazing transformation has taken place in the two
of us.

When we first married, we were as different as any
two people could be. Wayne was a night owl and I was a
morning person. Not only did I wake at the crack of dawn
(much to Wayne's annoyance), but I woke up happy. I liked
being around people, while he preferred solitude. And yet,

after all the years we've been together, our likes and dislikes have blended together. These days it isn't uncommon for us to order the same meal at a restaurant or choose to watch the same movie. Even our political views are the same. And though I'm still a morning person, Wayne seems to take it in stride.

In many ways, I've experienced the same kind of transformation in my walk with Jesus. As I've read my Bible and spent time in prayer, a subtle change has taken place within me: I want to be more like Him; I long for His power in my life.

Lord, may I grow more like You each and every day.

Today, Lord,
I read Habakkuk 3:17-19.
Endurance. The delays we endure
are not an accident.
They are part of Your plan
and purpose for us. These words
were written just for me today.
How patient You are with me, Father.
How loving and encouraging.
This time of testing is only a delay
to be used for Your purposes.

One of my favorite verses

I will be your God throughout your lifetime—
until your hair is white with age. I made you,
and I will care for you. I will carry you along and save you.

ISAIAH 46:4 (NLT)

> Oh, Timothy, my son, be strong with the strength
> Christ Jesus gives you. For you must teach
> others those things you and many others
> have heard me speak about.

—2 TIMOTHY 2:1–2 (TLB)

Because of my heavy travel schedule, routinely attending a Bible study is difficult for me. What I needed, I decided some years ago, was a spiritual mentor, someone who would guide me and be a sounding board for me, someone with a lot of spiritual maturity. I asked a godly woman in our church if she would be willing to meet and pray with me on a regular basis. That was how my friendship with Barb Dooley started. Even now, all these years later, we get together regularly to pray.

Recently I told Barb about a problem I'd been experiencing and the frustration I felt. "I don't know what

I'm doing wrong," I said. "I've filled up pages and pages in my prayer journal, pouring out my problem to God. I've brought the matter up daily, waiting for Him to move in my life. I don't think He hears my prayers any longer."

Barb didn't say anything for a long time. Then she smiled and said, "Maybe you should try a different tactic."

"How do you mean?" I said. I was open to anything.

Barb smiled and said softly, "Maybe this isn't a case of God not hearing your prayers, Debbie. I believe He's always available to His children. Perhaps He's just waiting for you to listen."

Father, open my heart so that I can hear
what You have to say to me.

Good morning, Lord.
May I choose a quiet heart, Father.
May I rest completely in You.
No matter what circumstances,
what befalls my life, may I see
and accept Your hand in it.
May I accept it with gratitude.
While the storms may rage
and the seas may churn,
let me sleep contentedly at Your side.

> *Find a good spouse, you find a good life—
> and even more: the favor of GOD!*
>
> —PROVERBS 18:22 (MSG)

Like most couples, Wayne and I have not had the perfect marriage. At one point we separated for nearly eighteen months before deciding that just wasn't the solution. Once we reunited, though, it wasn't smooth sailing. Old resentments surfaced, and I struggled with letting go of the pain from the past. One weekend I felt I needed to get away, and visiting my parents was the perfect excuse.

When I arrived, my mother insisted on picking up a bucket of her favorite chicken for dinner. For some reason she decided to drive. I climbed in the car with her, and she said, "Look behind me. Is anyone coming?"

I twisted around and checked. "You're clear."

"Great." She revved up the engine, and we shot out of the driveway and onto the street.

"Mom," I asked, suddenly suspicious, "can't you look behind you?"

"Good grief, no. I've had a crick in my neck for nearly twenty years." She proceeded to show me the elaborate way she twisted the rearview mirror to check for traffic behind her. I couldn't keep from smiling and joked with her about it.

The next day, as I was heading home, it struck me that God was speaking to me through my mother. She looked forward, not back. God seemed to be asking me to do the same: Concentrate on the present, look with faith toward the future and release the pain of the past.

Lord, I'm grateful for the miracles You've worked in my marriage, for the husband You gave me and for all the years we've shared together—the good with the bad. May we both look to You as we step toward the future.

One of my favorite verses

*Oh, what joy for those whose disobedience is forgiven,
whose sins are put out of sight. Yes, what joy for those
whose record the Lord has cleared of sin.*

ROMANS 4:7–8 (NLT)

Stitch by Stitch

I was only twelve years old when I decided that I wanted to knit. I pestered my mother until she took me to the local yarn store, and there I bought several skeins of yarn. Following the good advice of the ladies at the store, I knit my first garment—a purple vest of worsted wool—which I gave to my mother. I was so pleased with my work, and proud. Since then I have made sweaters, scarves, afghans, blankets, caps, Christmas stockings and maybe best of all, a sweater for the Guideposts Knit for Kids project. For years I knit only about one garment a year. But when the grandchildren started arriving, well, my knitting really took off.

Knitting is relaxing, even meditative, for me. I work hard as a novelist, holed up most of the day in my office, sitting at the keyboard, then making calls, e-mailing my editor and keeping up with my blog.

Then after dinner I take out my knitting and use it to relax and unwind while my husband Wayne and I talk or watch TV together. I'll knit just about anywhere—at home, during flights or in the car. It should be no surprise then that knitting has also taken a central spot in some of my fiction, with a passion for knitting bringing my characters together.

Recently I was reading from the Psalms, and the phrase that leaped out at me proclaimed how God "knit me together in my mother's womb." That image filled me with wonder at the care our Creator takes in shaping each one of us—no lost stitches anywhere! It made me see how the things I find most important in life are also reflected in my knitting.

> Recently I was reading from the Psalms,
> and the phrase that leaped out at me proclaimed how God
> "knit me together in my mother's womb."

So along with the sweaters and caps and scarves I knit for the grandchildren comes this advice: What's good for knitting is good for living.

Get hooked.

When I'm writing one of my books, I get so excited I can barely wait to get to work. Same thing for my knitting from the moment I envision a project until the very last stitch. Every time I start a sweater for one of the grandkids, I can't wait to pick up those needles. They call me Grandma Pickle (since Macomber sounds like Cucumber). When I'm finished I add little tags to the sweaters I knit that read, KNIT WITH LOVE BY GRANDMA PICKLE. They know who made that sweater for them and they know how much they're loved.

So do what you love and love what you do. It deserves your name on it.

Follow a pattern.

There are knitters who can sit down without a pattern and create beautiful things. Not me. I need to start out with some kind of plan. God can add all sorts of creative enhancements to make those plans better, but I have to begin with something. Give me a target, a goal to shoot for. If I know what I want, then I can figure out how to get there.

In my career and family life I have weekly goals—and daily ones too. Once a year, usually in January, I take one day and, together with Wayne, we set goals for the year. Sometimes they're such big goals they seem impossible to reach—but I'll put them down. Maybe not for the end of the year, but in five years or ten. And we pray over our list.

Not long ago I was clearing out a drawer and I found a tablet that I had written on back in 1992. I had placed five impossible goals on that list. When I saw that list so many years later, I was stunned. Every single goal on that piece of paper had come to pass!

Take it stitch by stitch.

I'm always amazed at the people I meet who have been knitting for years, yet they only knit scarves. They don't have the self-confidence to knit anything more complicated. What they don't realize is that every knitting project builds on the same basic stitches.

Most knitting is done in pieces. The project is created in stages, like building a house or writing a book. You don't have to do it all at once, but if you do a little bit every day, piece by piece, you'll be surprised at how much you can accomplish. I'm sure I don't need to point out that that's also true in many other aspects of our lives, faith especially. We get there, one stitch at a time.

Don't worry over every loose thread.

Neat, even stitches make for a well-crafted garment; stitches that are too tight look bunched up and stitches that are too loose...well, we've all seen those afghans with big holes in them where there shouldn't be any! We all make mistakes, but it's just as important to remember to continue and try again.

I remember when my daughter Jody was twelve years old and performing in a piano recital. She was shy around strangers, so recitals were torturous for her. This year she was forced to go first. I watched her go up onstage and sit down at the piano. She started her song tentatively and only a few measures into it, she made a mistake. A real clunker. She stopped. And she couldn't start again.

But at the end of the recital, when everybody had left the hall, I asked her gently if she would try again. She nodded, wiped her tears and went back onstage. She played the song perfectly! By the time she'd finished, everyone had come back into the hall, and gave her a big ovation. Making mistakes is part of getting it right.

Click together.

I was in an airport once, waiting to change planes, when I saw another woman at the gate, knitting. We immediately started talking and showing each other our projects. I discovered that the pattern she was knitting was the very pattern I had lost a few weeks before. When you spend time with people, you discover just how much you need their help.

Every winter Wayne and I drive from our home in Washington state down to our winter home in Florida. If you're wondering, that's 3,323 miles. We've endured a blizzard, breakdowns and have slept in towns where the biggest thing on Main Street was the car wash.

When you spend time with people,
you discover just how much you need their help.

People often ask us why we would choose to drive that far. The answer is simple: It's our one chance to be together for a whole week without any interruptions. It's amazing how much we have to discuss. Each year on that long drive from home to home we fall in love with each other all over again. It knits us together and, needless to say, gives me time to catch up on my many yarn projects!

Give it away.

One of the joys of knitting is giving to others. What am I going to do with a hundred sweaters? I certainly don't want to make them all for myself. I want to give them away to the people I love, or to a needy child in a cold corner of the world where a simple sweater is both a treasure and a necessity. To be sure, the best giving comes from the heart.

I think about that first purple vest I made for my mother all those years ago when I was twelve. I saw it a few times, but then it just went into a drawer. Well, she just died two years ago. Guess what? She still had that handmade, not-so-perfect but made-with-love worsted wool vest.

To be sure, the best giving comes from the heart.

Dear Lord,

my soul sings with Your praises this morning.

I sit where I can watch the sun rise

and hear the multitude of birds chirp,

welcoming each glorious day.

How I thank You for Your handiwork,

for new beginnings every twenty-four hours.

I thank You for the peace and assurance

that comes with the years of walking with my Savior.

My soul sings Your praises and rejoices

in the beauty of Your world.

Thank You for blessing my life

and for gently correcting and leading me.

May we always rejoice in Your handiwork.

Amen.

CHAPTER 3

Be a Blessing

Be a blessing. Three simple words, but what a profound impact we experience when we act on them. In our busy lives we often wonder how we are going to get through the to-do list, let alone bless other people. The good news is, it's easier than you might think. A chore done with a smile instead of a frown might be a blessing to our family. An encouraging word to a harried young mom or a gentle touch on the arm to a struggling senior may not take any time at all. If we look at each item on our list as a chance to bless someone, we not only affect others but we change our own lives.

> But among you it will be different. Whoever wants
> to be a leader among you must be your servant.
>
> —MATTHEW 20:26 (NLT)

I was always different as a child, when I so badly wanted to be like everyone else in my class. Because I'm dyslexic, I didn't start to read fluently until I was ten years old and in the fifth grade. My third-grade teacher told my mother, "Debbie's a nice little girl, but she's never going to do well in school." And I didn't; I struggled with poor grades all the way through school. College was never an option for me.

When I entered high school, my goal was to make the honor roll just once, for one quarter. I gave it my all. Not once did I make that list. On the last report card I received as a high-school senior, I was one point away.

I was different in other ways too. I wasn't pretty, and I struggled with my weight. I had only a few friends besides my cousins. I hated being so different.

Years later, after I started daily Bible reading, I discovered Matthew 20:26. Jesus is telling His disciples that to live the way He wants them to, they need to be servants. I read the verse another way. It was as if Jesus was telling me personally that He made me different for a reason: He had a purpose for me. Because I was different, I could encourage others to become all God intended.

None of us need allow our differences to hold us back in life. Our differences are reason to celebrate; after all, this is exactly the way God wanted us.

Thank You, Jesus, for making me different.

Lord, take my weakness
and turn it around
and make it my greatest strength.
I read that repentance is
simply changing our minds
about ourselves and our actions,
and seeing things God's way.
What profound words. Allow me
to see myself through Your eyes.
Let me hate sin in the same way
You do. Let me love obedience.
Let my struggle inspire others.
Let us work together.

*Be completely humble and gentle; be patient,
bearing with one another in love.*

—EPHESIANS 4:2 (NIV)

My husband and I both grew up in small towns. Colville, Washington, Wayne's hometown, had the only stoplight in the entire county when we married. Twenty-four years ago, when we moved to Port Orchard, there was only one stoplight in the entire city. Even now, neither one of us is accustomed to dealing with a lot of traffic. We know we're spoiled, and that's the way we like it.

When Jazmine, our oldest granddaughter, was around three years old, I picked her up in Seattle and drove her to Port Orchard. As luck would have it, I hit heavy traffic. For what seemed like hours we crawled at a snail's pace toward the Tacoma Narrows Bridge. In order to keep Jazmine entertained, I sang songs to her and made up silly stories. She chatted away happily in her car seat in the back, utterly content. Not so with me. My nerves were fried.

Finally I couldn't stand it any longer. "Jazmine, just look at all these cars," I muttered as I pressed on the horn. *What's the matter with these people anyway? Obviously, they don't realize I have places to go and people to see.* Normally the drive took only forty minutes, and I'd already been on the road an hour. "Grandma?" from the backseat came Jazmine's voice. "Are we in a hurry?"

Oh, Father, thank You for my sweet granddaughter and the reminder of what is really important: spending time with her.

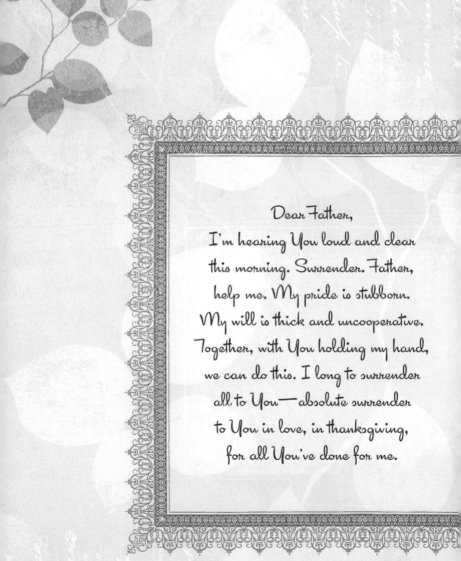

Dear Father,

I'm hearing You loud and clear
this morning. Surrender. Father,
help me. My pride is stubborn.
My will is thick and uncooperative.
Together, with You holding my hand,
we can do this. I long to surrender
all to You—absolute surrender
to You in love, in thanksgiving,
for all You've done for me.

Now your attitudes and thoughts must all be constantly changing for the better. Yes, you must be a new and different person, holy and good. Clothe yourself with this new nature.

—EPHESIANS 4:23–24 (TLB)

I have a notorious sweet tooth. Not only do I enjoy sampling desserts, I enjoy baking them and experimenting with recipes. People know they're in for a treat when we invite them to dinner. So it's no small sacrifice for me to give up sweets for Lent, which is something I've done for several years now.

This past Lent I had lunch with a friend, and when it came time to order dessert, she asked me what looked good.

"Everything," I told her and then explained that because it was Lent I was abstaining.

"Because of Lent?" she asked.

"Well, yes. Giving up something goes way back to my childhood. Don't you?"

"I used to," she explained, "but I've had a change of heart."

That intrigued me. "How do you mean?"

"Well," she said, "I decided that instead of giving up something, I would *do* something instead."

This was sounding better by the moment. "Give me an example," I said.

"I send a shut-in a card or make an overdue phone call to a friend or relative."

"That's great."

"At first it seems like a task, but I come away feeling better about life. I don't think it's a bad thing to give up something for Lent, but I've discovered that the things I do become habits and that makes a positive change in my life."

I'm looking to make positive changes in my life too. I'll continue to abstain from desserts during Lent because it's good for me and I appreciate them more at Easter, but from now on, I'm going to do something too.

Lord, open my eyes to the needs of others
and show me how I can make a difference
during Lent and all year round.

One of my favorite verses

I tell you the truth, anything you did for even the least of my people here, you also did for me.

MATTHEW 25:40 (NCV)

O taste and see that the LORD is good.

—PSALM 34:8 (KJV)

When our daughter Jody graduated from grade school, we decided to celebrate with dinner in a fancy restaurant. As we waited to be led to a table, I noticed the dessert platter filled with a variety of yummy temptations: cheesecake with strawberry topping; a thick, gooey chocolate cake; apple pie and much more. My husband Wayne asked me something, and I turned away from the platter. When I looked back, I noticed that someone had taken a bite out of each of the desserts!

My five-year-old Dale stared at me with a look of pure innocence, his mouth ringed with chocolate cake. I asked him why he would do such a thing, and he told me that he thought the platter was there so guests could sample the desserts before they ordered. Thankfully, the hostess was amused by my son's explanation, and we were all given dessert on the house.

Dale is a junior high school teacher now, and we like to tease him by telling him that he's the reason so many restaurants display plastic food instead of the real thing. But in retrospect, I think Dale might have been on to something: Reach out and taste life, or you might miss out on some of the wonderful experiences God has in store for you!

Father God, Your love overwhelms me.
Help me to be open to the opportunities You send my way.

Dearest Father,
someone prayed for me
and because of that prayer,
I am Your child this day.
At times I forget the
all-persuasive power of prayer
and how pleasing it is to You.
I've so often said to my children
that love equals time.
I need to remember that
proving my love for You
requires spending time with You.

One of my favorite verses

*As the Spirit of the Lord works within us, we become more
and more like him and reflect his glory even more.*

2 CORINTHIANS 3:18 (NLT)

> *Work willingly at whatever you do, as though you were working for the Lord rather than for people.*
>
> —COLOSSIANS 3:23 (NLT)

I've never had a lot of exposure to classical music, and I tend to listen to it without much appreciation. But I read a true story about a composer the other day that made me sit up and take notice.

Johann Sebastian Bach wrote each note as though God Himself was scrutinizing every musical bar and phrase. One of his most acclaimed works is *The Passion According to St. Matthew,* which has been called one of the greatest choral works ever written. Now here's what really got my attention: The *Passion* was performed only once while Bach was alive and wasn't all that well received. Just one performance. One.

Then a hundred years later, in 1829, Felix Mendelssohn obtained a copy from his teacher, who allegedly bought the original score from a merchant using it to wrap cheese. Mendelssohn's performance of the score was met with an appreciation and love that has never ebbed. This story certainly has God's fingerprints all over it.

What struck me particularly in the article, though, was this: At the beginning of almost all of his compositions, Bach wrote the abbreviation *JJ* for the Latin phrase *Jesu juva*, which means "Jesus help," and ended with *SDG* (*Soli Deo Gloria*), which is Latin for "To God Alone the Glory." This is just the reminder I need as I forge ahead in my life. All I do, every word I write, every action I take, everything belongs to God. To Him be the glory, always and forever.

Father, to You be the glory in all that I say and do.

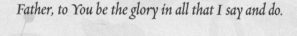

One of my favorite verses

*You keep your promises and show unfailing love
to all who obey you and are eager to do your will.*

2 Chronicles 6:14 (NLT)

He answered: "'Love the Lord your God with
all your heart and with all your soul and with
all your strength and with all your mind';
and, 'Love your neighbor as yourself.'"

—LUKE 10:27 (NIV)

For the past twenty years I've swum laps at the local high school pool. For those of us who gather in the pool lobby, there's nothing like the smell of chlorine in the morning to get our blood pumping. Over the years we've become good friends.

Recently, someone new joined our group. Arriving a bit later than the rest of us, she seemed to have trouble sharing the lane. She wanted her own space and started dishing out instructions. I heard plenty of grumbling about this newcomer. "Someone needs to tell Ms. Ponytail

about pool etiquette," I complained to the lifeguard. When I went in for my shower, I got an earful about the newbie who seemed to think the pool was her private property.

Back at home, I told my husband about the unpleasant woman who'd recently started swimming. Wayne asked me if I was going to invite her to our annual Swimmers' Tea.

I snorted softly and shook my head. "Hardly." She was the last person on my list. I couldn't imagine why Wayne would even suggest she be included.

The next morning, as I finished up my devotional time just before I changed into my swimsuit, I ran across a quote from Dorothy Day: "I really only love God as much as I love the person I love the least."

Hmm... It seemed God knew when to send me the message I needed the most. I looked at my invitation list for the Swimmers' Tea, sighed and added one additional name.

Father, thank You for every person You send my way,
even the prickly ones.

Dearest Father,
Your Word claims that
You love a cheerful giver.
May I always give You
my first and my best
and may I do it with a heart
full of joy and thanksgiving.
Not only the tithe of my earnings
but of my personal time
to reach others for You.

There are different kinds of gifts,
but the same Spirit. There are different kinds
of service, but the same Lord.

—1 CORINTHIANS 12:4–5 (NIV)

While my boys were in college, they struggled with what to buy their grandparents for Christmas. They wanted my mom and dad to know how much they loved them, but finding a gift within their price range became more of a challenge each year.

Then one Thanksgiving, my father casually mentioned how much he had loved decorating the house with lights every Christmas. He couldn't any longer and that saddened him.

Shortly afterward, Ted and Dale came to me with an idea. As their Christmas gift to their grandparents, they wanted to make the three-hour drive to their house and decorate it for Christmas.

I pitched in and purchased the necessary supplies, and the boys spent two days stringing up lights and boughs all around the outside of the house. Every bush, plant and tree trunk was wrapped in lights. My dad beamed with pride that his house was the most brilliantly lit home in the neighborhood.

Ted and Dale had such a good time with my parents, and each other, that they returned every couple of months and completed necessary tasks around the house that my father could no longer manage. My parents treasured this special gift more than anything the boys could have purchased.

I learned something valuable from my sons that year: An extra toy under the tree for the grandchildren won't mean half as much as playing a game with them or holding a special tea party complete with fancy hats and gloves. The gift of my time will be remembered long after they have outgrown their toys.

Lord Jesus, at the first Christmas You gave us the gift of Yourself. Help me to make myself a gift to others.

Lord, in reading the story
of Elisha and the widow's pot of oil,
it came to me that the oil flows
according to my faith. Let it flow,
Lord. Allow me to be a vessel
of blessing to all around me—
my family, my friends, my neighbors
and all who come into contact with me.
Let me be a blessing because I serve You.

Love each other with brotherly affection and take delight in honoring each other.

—ROMANS 12:10 (TLB)

In a recent sermon, our pastor Kevin mentioned an encounter he'd had with my husband Wayne. No one in church realized he was talking about Wayne, but I did.

Kevin had stopped by our house on a quick errand for his wife, and Wayne had asked him in for a cup of coffee. Kevin was in a hurry and declined; he had a meeting scheduled, places to go and people to see. Wayne didn't think anything of it and neither did I.

Then on Sunday morning Kevin talked about the incident. He said he had been so busy doing the *work* of the church that he'd forgotten to *be* the church. He'd missed an opportunity to get to know one of his flock better and he regretted it.

That set me to thinking about how many opportunities I've missed because I was in a hurry to get somewhere. How many people has God planted in my path whom I was in too much of a hurry to notice?

As an old saying has it, "You may be the only Bible someone will ever read." If that's the case, I want to make sure I represent the living Christ in a way that honors Him.

Father God, help me to live my life in such a way that
people will see my faith in the love I show others.

One of my favorite verses

I have told you all this so that you may have peace in me.
Here on earth you will have many trials and sorrows.
But take heart, because I have overcome the world.

JOHN 16:33 (NLT)

> *A soft answer turneth away wrath:*
> *but grievous words stir up anger.*
>
> —PROVERBS 15:1 (KJV)

My five-year-old-grandson Cameron was ready for his first day of kindergarten. I phoned my daughter Jenny after she dropped him off to catch the school bus.

"How did it go?" I asked. I knew Cameron was eager to start school, but both Jenny and I had our worries about our little Cam riding the big scary yellow bus on his own. "Another boy spat at him," Jenny told me and then went on to explain the circumstances. Both boys were in line waiting for the bus when some kind of disagreement broke out. Apparently the other boy didn't get his way and spat at Cameron.

My heart sank. I asked Jenny how she had handled the situation, since she was standing right there.

"I didn't need to do a thing. Cameron took care of it," Jenny explained. "He looked the boy directly in the eyes and said, 'If you do that, you can't be my friend.' By the time the bus arrived Cameron had a new friend. They had their arms around each other and were the best of buddies."

I was proud of my grandson's response to mistreatment, but at the same time I was reminded of how often I'm tempted to retaliate in kind when I feel wronged. Jesus calls me to live a life of love; my grandson gave me a beautiful example of how.

Dear Lord, help me always to follow Your—
and Cameron's—example and turn aside anger with love.

Dearest Lord,
give me a generous heart.
This is my prayer—the deep desire
of my heart. Help me to be open
to the suffering taking place
around me. Aware of others
who are hurting and in pain.
Don't allow me to be indifferent
to those in need but generous in heart,
attitude and deed.

> *For everyone who exalts himself will be humbled,
> and he who humbles himself will be exalted.*
>
> —LUKE 14:11 (NIV)

Medal of Honor recipient Bruce Crandall is a neighbor and a friend. He'll be the first one to say he's no hero. The way Bruce tells it, the real heroes didn't come home. He is the last Medal of Honor recipient to receive the medal in person; all the medals since Vietnam have been presented posthumously.

Recently, my husband Wayne and I were on a flight with Bruce that landed in Atlanta. Anyone who travels frequently knows what happens when the airplane door opens: There's a mad rush to get off and hurry to baggage claim or to a connecting flight. In Atlanta, there are a lot of connecting flights.

When it was discovered that a Medal of Honor recipient was aboard, the flight attendant asked the passengers to remain in their seats and allow Bruce to deplane first. I've heard such announcements before, and they're routinely ignored.

Not this time. Everyone aboard the plane remained seated. Then, as Bruce stood and collected his carry-on, a spontaneous burst of applause broke out. As he disembarked, Bruce paused to let three young recruits headed for basic training leave ahead of him.

As I said, Bruce would be the last one to say he's a hero, but I can't help viewing him that way. He's the very best of what it means to be an American.

Lord, thank You for the people who remind us
of the tremendous cost the men and women of our military
have paid for our freedom.

One of my favorite verses

I leave you peace; my peace I give you. I do not give it to you as the world does. So don't let your hearts be troubled.

JOHN 14: 27 (NCV)

> I will make you into a great nation
> and I will bless you; I will make your name great,
> and you will be a blessing.

— GENESIS 12:2 (NIV)

I've been a member of the Peale Center's Positive Thinkers Club for the last seventeen years. A few years back, Ruth Stafford Peale wrote about simplifying our lives. The first step in making that leap is to determine what is really important to each one of us. One way to accomplish this is to create a mission statement.

I'd been thinking about creating such a statement for a long while, but I had put it off. I'd toyed with a number of ideas, but they felt clumsy and wordy. When I'm stuck, what sometimes works best for me is to put things aside and let the Lord direct me.

It shouldn't come as any surprise, but I found the answer in my Bible. I was reading Genesis 12, where God makes His covenant with Abram. God tells Abram that He will make him into a great nation and that He will bless him. The last part of verse 2 was what caught my eye: "You will be a blessing." I read those words twice as they gripped my heart. This was my mission statement, simple, profound and direct.

Thank You, heavenly Father, for directing my path and showing me how You want me to live.

Beloved, I pray that you may prosper in all things
and be in health, just as your soul prospers.

—3 John 1:2 (NKJV)

For years a group of us at First Christian Church of Port Orchard, Washington, have made prayer shawls for people in the congregation. It's our way of showing them God is always near. This past winter I wondered who else to knit for. What about our high school seniors? Soon they'd be going off to college. I remembered how worried I'd been when our kids left home. Would they make the right choices? Hold fast to their values?

"Let's knit for our high school seniors," I suggested to the group. "We could do afghans for the boys and shawls for the girls." The other women loved my idea! We worked all winter, every stitch a prayer for the grad-to-be.

On graduation weekend, our seven seniors will receive an afghan or shawl, a reminder that no matter how far away they go for college, the love and prayers of people back home go with them.

Dearest Father,

may my light shine for You all the days
of my life and glow for many years after.
May all the good that I attempt
in Your name give glory to You.
Because of Your love, my own spills over
onto others. I long to touch lives for You,
to show others the way to companionship with You,
to link others' lives to You so they can
make a difference. Let us be a blessing.

Amen.

CHAPTER 4

Thank-You Notes to God

Several years ago I adopted the Quaker practice of keeping a gratitude journal. Each day I would write down five things for which I was thankful. I started out writing the expected things—family, friends, God's provision—but as the years went on I dug deeper. I learned how to be thankful for the bumps in the road, the struggles, even the tragedies. This practice changed my life. Yes, offering thanks to God for all the good things He brings to us is important, but the act of practicing gratitude in all things is the very antidote to despair.

When life is heavy and hard to take,
go off by yourself. Enter the silence. Bow in prayer.
Don't ask questions: Wait for hope to appear.
Don't run from trouble. Take it full-face.
The "worst" is never the worst.

—LAMENTATIONS 3:28–30 (MSG)

My walking partner Martha is sassy, irreverent and just plain fun, so it was something of a shock to see tears in her eyes when we met up one day.

"We lost everything in the stock market," she explained. Martha and her husband are both retired and live on their investment income. Their entire nest egg was gone and Martha was devastated.

To my surprise, she met me the following morning with a big smile. "It's going to be okay," she said. Her sister had e-mailed her a note that said, "If God brings you to it, He will see you through it." The message lingered in her mind, and later that day as she shopped in a local department store, the most amazing thing happened. Martha had stopped to look at a ring on a counter display. It took her a moment to realize the inside of the ring had an inscription. It read: "If God brings you to it, He will see you through it."

While Martha badly needed the reassurance God offered her that day, it was something I needed to be reminded of too: God is our Father. He willingly, lovingly supplies all my needs. No matter what happens in my life, He will always be at my side.

You fulfill my every need, Father. May I always
turn to You instead of relying on my own resources,
no matter what the situation.

One of my favorite verses

I am convinced that nothing can ever separate us from God's love.
Neither death nor life, neither angels nor demons,
neither our fears for today, our worries about tomorrow,
and even the powers of hell can't keep God's love away.

ROMANS 8:38 (NLT)

May he give you the desire of your heart
and make all your plans succeed.

—PSALM 20:4 (NIV)

Several years ago I compiled a list of thirty people I wanted to meet. Since then I've met nineteen of them, including writers, musicians and actors. Inspired by my success, my son Dale decided to make a list of his own. Unfortunately, the one person he wanted most to meet was Steve Prefontaine, the legendary runner who was killed in a car accident twenty-three days before Dale was born. Dale has read Steve's life story many times. Every term paper or school project he was assigned, from the time he was in grade school all the way through college, revolved around some aspect of Steve's life.

Because he knew it would be impossible to meet his hero, Dale and his best friend Andy, both runners themselves, decided to celebrate Steve's birthday in a unique way: They would visit all the key locations of his life on Steve's birthday, January 31. They started off by visiting Marshfield High in Coos Bay, Oregon, where Steve went to school, and ran around the track that's named after him. They toured the museum with Steve's memorabilia and then stopped off to visit his gravesite. On the way out of town, they decided to take pictures of the house where Steve's parents lived. While they were outside, a man stopped and asked them what they were doing.

"Did you know this is the house where Steve Prefontaine's parents lived when he was born?" Dale asked enthusiastically.

"As a matter of fact, I do," the older man told them. "I'm Steve's father."

Mr. Prefontaine took Dale and Andy inside the house and showed them their hero's bedroom. They tried on Steve's letterman's jacket and had their pictures taken in it. This proud father gave my son and his best friend the thrill of their lives.

Dale and Andy came as close as it is possible this side of heaven to meeting their hero.

Oh, we serve a mighty God,
Who delights in giving us the desires of our hearts.

One of my favorite verses

I am the Good Shepherd; I know my own sheep and they know me.

JOHN 10:14 (NLT)

You alone are the LORD. You made the heavens,
even the highest heavens, and all their starry host,
the earth and all that is on it,
the seas and all that is in them.

—Nehemiah 9:6 (NIV)

When my oldest granddaughter Jazmine was about fourteen months old, a circus came to our area. I thought that it would be something she'd enjoy, and so her mother Jody and I drove down to the local fairgrounds where the circus had pitched its tent.

After buying our tickets, we made our way into the grandstand, where Jazmine sat on my lap. At first she clung to me, frightened by all the strange sights and sounds. Then the elephant with his trainer stepped into view. Jazmine's eyes widened with awe as the huge, lumbering beast made its way into the center ring.

"Look at his big ears," I said, pointing. "And his long, long nose."

Jazmine stared at the elephant for a moment and a look of rapture spread over her face. Then she started to applaud, her small hands bouncing against each other in an outburst of joy. She laughed and cheered, and soon I was laughing and cheering too. Jazmine's delight became my own.

Sometime later I paused to watch the sun set in a pink and orange sky. Golden light radiated from the horizon. The view was spectacular. I caught my breath and then, following my granddaughter's example, I looked up to heaven and applauded.

Lord, may I always maintain a childlike wonder
as I view the world You made.

Dearest Lord,
thank You for Your creative hand
in the animal kingdom and all the
lessons we can learn from them.
Only yesterday I read in Proverbs
about the ant that gathers food
in winter, industrious, hard-working,
concerned for her family.
Today I'll pay more attention
to Your creatures and appreciate
Your hand on all life.

One of my favorite verses

Be still and know that I am God!

PSALM 46:10 (NLT)

He calls his own sheep by name and leads them.

—JOHN 10:3 (NIV)

Wayne and I chose a family name for the middle names of each of our four children. Jody Rose, our oldest daughter, was named for my mother; Jenny Adele was named for Wayne's mother. Later, as Jody grew, it became apparent that she resembled Wayne's side of the family far more than mine. My blonde, blue-eyed daughter was all Macomber. Jenny, on the other hand, with her dark hair and eyes, resembled the Adler side of the family. It seemed to us that we'd picked the wrong names for the girls.

The thought was even stronger when Jody entered her teens and often clashed with my mom. As Jody matured, however, her relationship with my mother mellowed and the two grew especially close.

Shortly after my father died, we moved Mom to an assisted-living complex in Port Orchard, Washington, where we live. It was Jody who stopped by the complex two or three times a week to visit Mom; it was Jody who took her to her doctor's appointments if I was out of town; and it was Jody who sat with Mom and me after Mom suffered a stroke and slipped into a coma. During Mom's final minutes on earth, it was Jody who sat by my side and prayed with me as God's angels ushered Mom into glory.

At the funeral, as my daughter offered the eulogy, I sat with tears in my eyes. Wayne and I had given our daughter the right name after all. God knew all along that she was meant to be Jody Rose.

Father God, how grateful I am that
You know us all better than we know ourselves.

Dearest Father,
I read that when we say,
"The Lord is my Shepherd,"
it carries the confession of our own
helplessness and need of a
Shepherd's care. Without You,
I am a lost sheep, caught in
a rocky steep, snared and vulnerable
until You seek me out and rescue me.
Oh, Father, I know that even in my
depraved condition I am
Your sheep—one of Your flock—
and You will come for me.

One of my favorite verses

Death is swallowed up in victory. O death, where is your victory?
O death, where is your sting?

1 CORINTHIANS 15:54–55 (NLT)

> *For where your treasure is,*
> *there your heart will be also.*
>
> —LUKE 12:34 (NIV)

I had lunch recently with my friend Sandy O'Donnell. Sandy told me that she'd recently sent her college-age daughter Shannon the Bible Shannon had used as a child. Sandy's eyes twinkled as she confessed, "I put three crisp twenty-dollar bills between the pages of Shannon's old Bible. She doesn't know they're there, and I'm wondering how long it will take her to find them."

Treasures buried in God's Word. I loved it.

I was already a young mother before I discovered the treasures in the Bible. After attending my first Bible study, I came away feeling like the richest woman in the world.

That feeling continues to this day. Every time I read the Bible, I find new treasures on each page.

I travel a lot, and I'm often in hotel rooms. So I've started a new habit: Inspired by Sandy, I reach for the Gideon Bible, open it, and place a twenty-dollar bill inside. I want whoever finds it to realize that there are other treasures waiting there to be discovered.

Lord, thank You for the treasures of Your Word,
precious beyond price.

Dearest, dearest Father,
my heart is so full of Your love
it feels it could burst wide open.
I serve a wonder-doing God.
A God Who's only limited by
my expectations. A God Who
loves me, encourages me,
cheers me, guides me
and speaks to me. You are awesome,
Father. I praise Your name
forever and ever.

> And over all these virtues put on love,
> which binds them all together in perfect unity.
>
> —COLOSSIANS 3:14 (NIV)

When I was a child and my father traveled out of town, I remember asking him to bring me a surprise from wherever he was going. I looked forward to his return eagerly, wondering what he was bringing back for me. In fact, unlike some people I know, I actually enjoy surprises...well, most of the time.

A number of years ago my daughters Jody and Jenny decided to throw me a surprise fiftieth birthday party. They spared no expense. In fact, they rented a hall, hired a catering company to serve a buffet dinner and planned an elaborate program that included speeches by teachers, editors I've worked with and high school friends.

Because the details of arranging the party became too much for them, they asked for my help. They brought the guest list to me to go over and needed some guidance on the decorations and music. Actually, I was a bit taken aback when the invitation announced it as a surprise party because by this point I knew practically every detail.

"Why are you calling it a surprise party?" I asked. I certainly wasn't going to appear shocked when I'd personally selected every name on the invitation list. In fact, I'd chosen the dinner menu and helped order the cake.

"Mom," Jenny said, beaming me a smile, "the surprise is you get to pay for it."

Thank You, Jesus, for the joy of my children
and the surprises they bring.

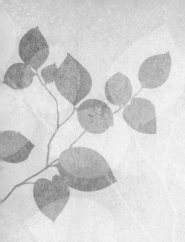

How wonderful are Your promises,
Father, and Your ways. I thank You
for my parents and know that
the woman I am this day
is a tribute to them. I forgive them
their faults and pray they can
forgive me mine. By the same token,
I pray my children will be
generous in forgiving me.

One of my favorite verses

*I will make you into a great nation. I will bless you
and make you famous and you will be a blessing to others.*

GENESIS 12:2 (NLT)

The LORD will guide you always;
he will satisfy your needs in a sun-scorched land
and will strengthen your frame.

—Isaiah 58:11 (NIV)

My husband's best friend Norm fell from the roof of his house. Complications from his injuries set in, and he wasn't expected to live through the night. Distraught, Norm's family gathered at the hospital. Not wanting to intrude on their privacy, Wayne and I felt there was little we could do but pray as we awaited word.

Feeling the need to do more in some way, Wayne asked me to contact our church to ask if one of the pastors could go to the hospital and pray with the family. The assistant pastor went and reported back that he'd met the family, shared the gospel and prayed with them. He mentioned how receptive and grateful they were for his visit. Later when we got news that Norm had miraculously survived the night, Wayne and I were overwhelmed with joy. But when I mentioned our pastor's visit to Norm's wife Sharon, she sounded confused. No one from the church had stopped by to visit or pray with them. We learned that the pastor had met with a different grieving family. As it happened, their family member died that night.

Some might say that our assistant pastor made a mistake, but I don't believe it.

God sent our pastor to the people who needed Him most.

Thank You, Lord, that You know
our needs and are always ready to meet them.

One of my favorite verses

Therefore, since we have been made right in God's sight
by faith, we have peace with God because of what
Jesus Christ our Lord has done for us.

ROMANS 5:1 (NLT)

172

But for that very reason I was shown mercy
so that in me, the worst of sinners,
Christ Jesus might display his unlimited
patience as an example for those who would
believe on him and receive eternal life.

—1 TIMOTHY 1:16 (NIV)

I'm seldom idle; my schedule is packed with meetings, travel and appointments. When I do sit down, I have either a pair of knitting needles in my hand or a book. I'm not a patient person; it's simply not in my genetic makeup to gaze at a sunset for more than a few pleasurable moments. It's lovely, but there's dinner to cook and things that need to be done.

But last year I injured my rotator cuff and needed surgery. The surgeon said I'd need six to eight weeks to heal properly and several months of physical therapy. I listened and nodded at all the right times, but I figured I'd be back in the office within a week or two. I was wrong.

I tried to work, but my energy level was so low that after a short while I needed a nap. Surely the Lord knew about my deadlines; didn't He care about the commitments I'd made and the people who relied on me?

After five weeks of staying at home, attending physical therapy three days a week and napping every day, I'm here to tell you that God does care. The time at home rejuvenated my marriage, inspired my creativity and gave me a renewed appreciation of life.

Lord, I'm grateful that You're never idle in Your care for me.

Dearest Father,
I remember reading one time—
years ago now—that if God
feels far away, we need to
ask ourselves, "Who moved?"
There have been times in my life
when I felt utterly alone
but You have always stood
at my side and guided me—
always walked each step with me.
Thank You.

> Don't you see that children are God's best gift?
> the fruit of the womb his generous legacy?...
> Oh, how blessed are you parents,
> with your quivers full of children!
>
> —Psalm 127:3, 5 (MSG)

Wayne and I have been blessed with four children and eight grandchildren. Without prejudice I can state that each child is intelligent, gifted, charming, clever, funny...you get the idea. Needless to say, we are proud parents. And don't get me started on the grandkids; they are by far the cutest ones in the universe, but I understand this is a title they share with many others.

Over the years I've been asked if any of my children will become writers. They certainly could, seeing that each one is creative and talented. But none of them has a passion to get published.

Recently, though, our eight-year-old grandson James wrote a story in his third-grade class that showed real writing ability. Like many good writers, he based his story on a true incident. A few months earlier, his grade school had been broken into and vandalized, with damages totaling several thousand dollars. Sadly, the culprits were never found or prosecuted. This bothered James, so he wrote about it.

God, thank You for the small encouragements
You send into my life. Help me to celebrate the little steps
I take as I trudge toward my goal.

Good morning, Lord.
"Go forward with an enlarged heart."
Those words jumped out at me
from my devotional reading
this morning—their meaning simple
and, at the same time, profound.
I am to move forward in my walk
with my Savior. And I am to do so
with a heart so full of love that
it becomes engorged with the emotion.

One of my favorite verses

The LORD is my strength and shield. I trust him
with all my heart. He helps me, and my heart is filled with joy.
I burst out in songs of thanksgiving.

PSALM 28:7 (NLT)

> *There is rejoicing in the presence*
> *of the angels of God over one sinner who repents.*
>
> —LUKE 15:10 (NIV)

Our daughter Jody asked me to watch her cat Jake-O over the weekend while she was out of town. I didn't mind, although Jake-O was spoiled and fussy. From the moment Jody left him with me, he either hissed at me or hid beneath the sofa.

My day brightened when my husband Wayne, who'd been out of town, arrived home early. I rushed outside to greet him and in my excitement left the front door open. Seeing his opportunity, Jake-O, who'd never been outside and had been declawed, shot out the door and into the woods.

Wayne and I searched for hours. We offered a reward

for anyone who would return him to us. But by the end of the day, we'd given up hope.

That night all I could think about was poor Jake-O. In a strange environment he'd be unable to find his way back to the house. Without claws he had no way to protect himself and some forest creature was sure to kill him. As I lay in bed, sick at heart, I prayed that the angels would watch over him.

Eventually I fell asleep, but my dreams were filled with Jake-O. I woke to the faint and distant cry of a...*Could it be a cat?* Disoriented, I raced down the hallway. Sure enough, it was Jake-O. He was on the second-story windowsill, peering at me through the glass.

Wayne joined me, and we both marveled at how Jake-O had gotten up so high. Jokingly, Wayne suggested that perhaps an angel had planted him there. I remembered my prayer and smiled.

"You know, sweetheart, you just might be right."

*Lord, thank You for caring about those who are lost
and for rejoicing when one of them is found,
even if it's a fussy cat named Jake-O.*

Safe in the Storm

I poured myself a cup of tea and waited anxiously by the phone. Everyone likes a white Christmas, but this was ridiculous. Over thirty inches had fallen on Port Orchard in under forty-eight hours, and the snow showed no signs of letting up. My parents had left our house early yesterday morning. The drive to Yakima was almost two hundred miles. They'd hoped to make it home before the worst of the storm hit, but after two hours on the road they'd only reached North Bend.

"Snoqualmie Pass is closed," Mom reported to me from a phone in a diner. "They're worried about avalanches. As soon as it opens we'll be on our way."

We kept in touch throughout the day. The snow kept falling. Mom and Dad had been stuck in the diner all night. "Thank goodness there's a pay phone there," I told my husband Wayne. "At least we know what's happening."

God, please let me know they're okay.

The phone finally rang again. I put down my tea and answered. Mom's voice sounded tired. "Your dad's not doing well," she said. "Neither of us slept much. The Red Cross is evacuating us to a school. They have blankets and food, but there's no phone there so you won't hear from us for a while."

I never should have let them leave here, I thought as I hung up. Hours went by. No word from Mom and Dad. "Mom said Dad wasn't feeling well," I told Wayne that evening. "What if it's his heart? He could have another heart attack. And Mom sounded exhausted. If only I knew they were okay."

"They'll get in touch soon," Wayne assured me. He turned on the TV. I sat on the edge of my chair, not wanting to miss a word about the storm, the Pass, the roads. The damage was astonishing: roofs caved in, marinas sunk. *God, please let me know they're okay.*

That Christmas I knew God was in charge—
no matter where they were.

"Now to some folks who have been stranded in North Bend," the announcer said. The news rolled footage of a school full of kids, rescue workers, moms and…"Dad!" I said. There he was, playing pinochle with other men, looking well. The camera panned the room and I saw Mom, leading a group in Christmas carols.

It was another day before my parents were able to cross Snoqualmie Pass. But I wasn't worried. That Christmas I knew God was in charge—no matter where they were.

Dearest Jesus,
thankfulness is a journey
I've been traveling for many years now
and I still have a long,
long way to traverse.
I don't know if it's humanly possible
to thank You for all that You've
done in my life and in the life
of my family. My heart is full of love
and thanksgiving to You.

Father,

I am reminded of Genesis 35:3,
"I will make there an altar unto God,
who answered me in the day of my distress."
I thank You for the altars in my own life—
the places where we have met
that bring my heart soaring to You.
This old kitchen chair where I sit each
morning for my devotions—where I write
my thank-you notes to You—is an example.
This is our meeting place, Yours and mine,
where I bring my cares and joys to my Father,
my Friend, my Comforter. Help us all recognize
those meeting places in our lives.

Amen.

Twenty-five (er, make that twenty-six!) of my favorite books

FICTION

The Secret Garden by Frances Hodgson Burnett
The Lion, the Witch and the Wardrobe by C. S Lewis
So Big by Edna Ferber
My Antonia by Willa Cather
A Good Earth by Pearl S. Buck
Little Women by Louisa May Alcott
Pride and Prejudice by Jane Austen
To Kill a Mockingbird by Harper Lee
Pillars of the Earth by Ken Follett
Mrs. Mike by Benedict and Nancy Freedman
The March by E. L. Doctorow
Exodus by Leon Uris

NONFICTION

The Christian's Secret of a Happy Life by Hannah Whitall Smith
The Power of Positive Thinking by Norman Vincent Peale
What in the World Is Going On? (and many others) by Dr. David Jeremiah
Heaven Is for Real by Todd Burpo
Your Best Life Now by Joel Osteen
Becoming a Contagious Christian by Bill Hybels
Getting Through the Tough Stuff (and just about everything else written) by Charles Swindoll
The Confident Woman by Joyce Myers
25 Ways to Win with People (and dozens of others) by John Maxwell
The Hiding Place by Corrie ten Boom
The Prayer of Jabez (and so many others) by Bruce Wilkinson
A Grief Observed by C. S. Lewis
The Ragamuffin Gospel by Brennan Manning
The Diary of Anne Frank by Anne Frank

About the Author

Debbie Macomber continues to top the fiction bestseller lists. Three of her novels have scored the number-one slot on the *New York Times*, *USA Today* and *Publishers Weekly* lists the first week on sale. When not writing, she enjoys knitting, traveling with her husband Wayne and putting on Grandma Camps for her grandchildren, for whom she has built a four-star tree house behind her home in Port Orchard, Washington.

A Note from the Editors

We hope you enjoy *Patterns of Grace*, created by Guideposts Books and Inspirational Media. In all of our books, magazines and outreach efforts, we aim to deliver inspiration and encouragement, help you grow in your faith and celebrate God's love in every aspect of your daily life.

Thank you for making a difference with your purchase of this book, which helps fund our many outreach programs to the military, prisons, hospitals, nursing homes and schools. Visit GuidepostsFoundation.org to learn more.

We also maintain many useful and uplifting online resources. Visit Guideposts.org to read true stories of hope and inspiration, access Our Prayer network, sign up for free newsletters, join our Facebook community and subscribe to our stimulating blogs.

To order your favorite Guideposts publication, go to ShopGuideposts.org, call (800) 932-2145 or write to Guideposts, PO Box 5815, Harlan, Iowa 51593.